Pebble® Plus

First Ladies

Jacqueline Kennedy

by Lucia Raatma

Consulting editor: Gail Saunders-Smith, PhD

Consultant: Carl Sferrazza Anthony, Historian
National First Ladies' Library
Canton, Ohio

CAPSTONE PRESS
a capstone imprint

Pebble Plus is published by Capstone Press,
151 Good Counsel Drive, P.O. Box 669, Mankato, Minnesota 56002.
www.capstonepub.com

032010
005740CGF10

Books published by Capstone Press are manufactured with paper containing at least 10 percent post-consumer waste.

Library of Congress Cataloging-in-Publication Data
Raatma, Lucia.
    Jacqueline Kennedy / by Lucia Raatma.
    p. cm.—(Pebble plus. First ladies)
    Summary: "Simple text and photographs describe the life of Jacqueline Kennedy"—Provided by publisher.
    Includes bibliographical references and index.
    ISBN 978-1-4296-5009-0 (library binding)
    ISBN 978-1-4296-5601-6 (paperback)
    1. Onassis, Jacqueline Kennedy, 1929-1994—Juvenile literature. 2. Presidents' spouses—United
States—Biography—Juvenile literature. I. Title.
E843.K4R27 2011
973.922092—dc22
[B]   2009050355

Editorial Credits
Jennifer Besel, editor; Ashlee Suker, designer; Svetlana Zhurkin, media researcher;
    Eric Manske, production specialist

Photo Credits
Corbis/Bettmann, 5, 6–7, 11, 16–17; Reuters/Jim Bourg, 21
Getty Images/CBS Photo Archive, 1, 13; Central Press, 19; Time & Life Pictures/George Silk, cover (right)
John Fitzgerald Kennedy Library, Boston/White House/Cecil Stoughton, 9; White House/Robert Knudsen, 15
Shutterstock/Alaettin Yildirim, 5, 7, 9, 11, 17, 19, 21 (caption plate); antoninaart, cover (left), 1, 8–9, 22–23, 24 (pattern);
    Gemenacom, 9 (frame)

Note to Parents and Teachers

The First Ladies series supports national history standards related to people and culture. This book describes and illustrates the life of Jacqueline Kennedy. The images support early readers in understanding the text. The repetition of words and phrases helps early readers learn new words. This book also introduces early readers to subject-specific vocabulary words, which are defined in the Glossary section. Early readers may need assistance to read some words and to use the Table of Contents, Glossary, Read More, Internet Sites, and Index sections of the book.

Table of Contents

Early Life

Jacqueline Kennedy

was a popular first lady.

She was born

on July 28, 1929,

in Southampton, New York.

Her parents were Janet

and John Bouvier.

born in Southampton,
New York

1929

Young Jackie
with her mother
in 1933

Jackie enjoyed writing
and painting. She also liked
learning about other countries.
In 1947 Jackie started at
Vassar College.
After college she became
a newspaper reporter.

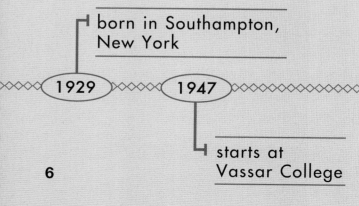

born in Southampton,
New York

1929   1947

starts at
Vassar College

Jackie in 1952, taking a picture for a newspaper article

7

In 1953 Jackie married

John Kennedy.

He was a U.S. senator

from Massachusetts.

They had four children.

But two of the children

died as babies.

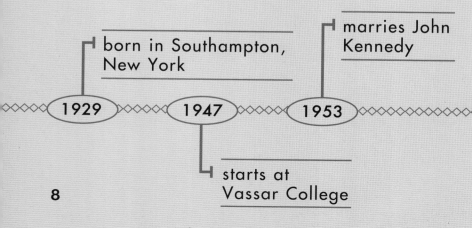

born in Southampton,
New York

marries John
Kennedy

1929   1947   1953

starts at
Vassar College

Jackie and John
with their children,
John Jr. (left) and
Caroline (right)

First Lady

In 1961 John became

president of the United States.

Jackie became first lady.

She traveled

to many countries.

She spoke in French, Italian,

and Spanish.

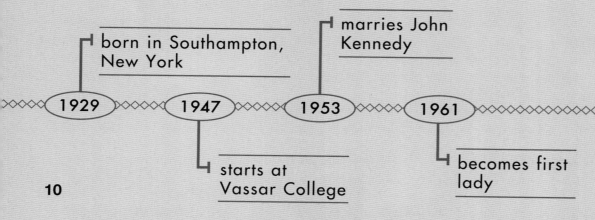

born in Southampton,
New York

marries John
Kennedy

1929   1947   1953   1961

starts at
Vassar College

becomes first
lady

In 1961 Jackie gave a speech in Spanish while visiting Venezuela.

As first lady, Jackie organized
the art in the White House.
She hired a person
to keep track of all the art
and furniture. She helped
make the first catalog
of White House art.

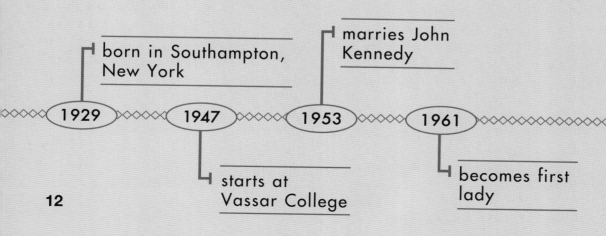

born in Southampton,
New York

marries John
Kennedy

1929   1947   1953   1961

starts at
Vassar College

becomes first
lady

People liked Jackie's style.

She wore small hats

and beautiful clothes.

Women copied her clothing

and hairstyle.

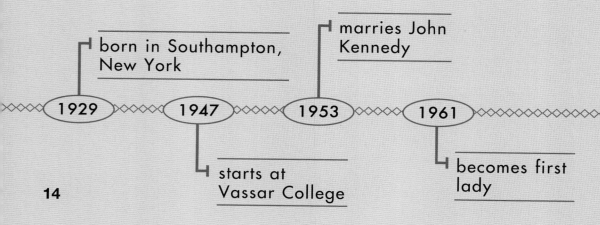

1929 — born in Southampton, New York

1947 — starts at Vassar College

1953 — marries John Kennedy

1961 — becomes first lady

After the White House

John was assassinated in 1963. Jackie and her children moved to New York City. Being a good mother was very important to her.

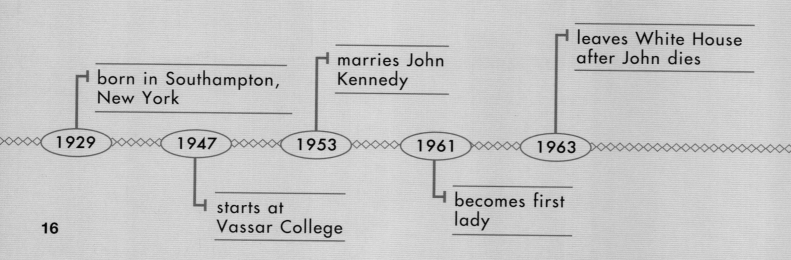

1929 — born in Southampton, New York

1947 — starts at Vassar College

1953 — marries John Kennedy

1961 — becomes first lady

1963 — leaves White House after John dies

Jackie and her children loved riding horses.

17

In 1968 Jackie married

Aristotle Onassis.

He was a businessman

from Greece.

They had homes in New York

and Greece.

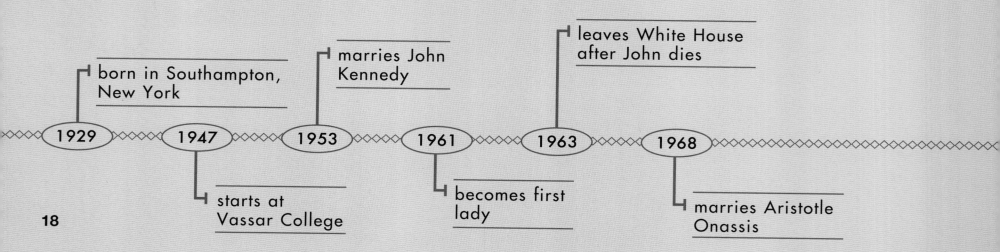

born in Southampton,
New York

marries John
Kennedy

leaves White House
after John dies

1929   1947   1953   1961   1963   1968

starts at
Vassar College

becomes first
lady

marries Aristotle
Onassis

Aristotle and Jackie in 1968

After Aristotle died
Jackie began working
as a book editor.
In 1994 Jackie died of
cancer. She is remembered
for her love of art, words,
and history.

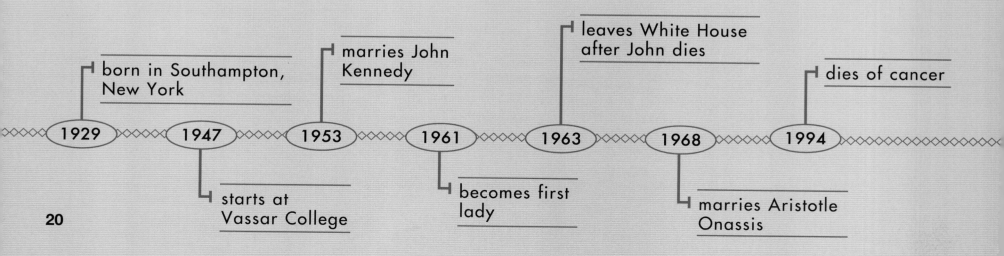

born in Southampton,
New York

marries John
Kennedy

leaves White House
after John dies

dies of cancer

1929   1947   1953   1961   1963   1968   1994

starts at
Vassar College

becomes first
lady

marries Aristotle
Onassis

Jackie with her two grown children in 1992

Glossary

assassinate—to murder a person who is well known or powerful

catalog—a book or list that shows works of art

editor—a person who checks the contents of a book and gets it ready to be published

first lady—the wife of the president of the United States

popular—liked by many people

senator—a person who serves in the Senate, making laws

style—the way a person dresses

Read more

Jones, Veda Boyd. *John F. Kennedy*. Rookie Biographies. New York: Children's Press, 2006.

Kennedy, Marge. *See inside the White House*. Scholastic News Nonfiction Readers. New York: Children's Press, 2009.

Mattern, Joanne. *Jacqueline Kennedy*. First Ladies. Edina, Minn.: Abdo Publishing, 2008.

Internet Sites

FactHound offers a safe, fun way to find Internet sites related to this book. All of the sites on FactHound have been researched by our staff.

Here's all you do:

Visit *www.facthound.com*

FactHound will fetch the best sites for you!

Index

Word Count: 222
Grade: 1
Early-Intervention Level: 20